AuthorHouse™
1663 Liberty Drive
Bloomington, IN 47403
www.authorhouse.com
Phone: 1-800-839-8640

Published by AuthorHouse 07/21/2015

ISBN: 978-1-4969-5426-8 (sc)

Library of Congress Control Number: 2014921906

Print information available on the last page.

For Information, Contact
bettymay88@gmail.com
www.bettymay2020.com

authorHOUSE

THE Chinese
REGIONAL GOURMET
COOKBOOK

Chinese Cooking, Ancient & Modern, for the 21st Century

By

BETTY MAY

THE CHINESE REGIONAL GOURMET COOKBOOK

Betty is a multi-talented person who shares a genuine passion and skill for cooking. She committed to every part of her work, and is diligent in her aspiration to be excellent in every aspect of cooking. As she writes this cook book, she does not only present the methods of cooking, but also motivate the readers to discover and enjoy the small joys of life.
Kenneth Kwan, President of Bright Hope Education and Community Center

"Blessed by God with her gifts in cooking, dancing, and photography, Betty May an exceptionally well-rounded individual. Tasting her refined Chinese dishes brings joy to all those who taste it. Her mastery of these delicacies is a sublimation of "the art of cooking."
Gary Tam, Cell Group Zone Leader

From scientists come discovery, inventors creativity, and artists beauty, but from chefs come creative ways to make food beautiful to behold yet delicious at the same time. While her creations are beautiful and intricate, no one in our group could deny himself a taste of Betty's handiwork. I wish you the same savory experience as you work through her book.
Samuel Chang, Pastor

Betty May is a very arty legend and passion for life, the life like an amazing painting colorful fine art to her. All food after her magic touch will turn into eye candy beautiful, delicious and the dish she prepare are spectacular memorable.
Sue Wang, Vineyard of Harvest Church

Since I met and knowing Betty, her life is full of love, she is a multi talented artist, not only a good person, she is a down to earth person, perfect food experts and a great teacher, this Chinese Cook Book will brought you authentic and contemporary Chinese recipes for you to enjoy cooking, and improve your cooking skill.
Shirley Hsieh, VOH

Betty May has been our friend and neighbor for many years. We admire her many talents when it comes to cooking, dancing, or flower arrangements. She excels in all of these fields but when it comes to Chinese Cooking she surpasses them all. Betty also knows the importance of giving back to her community through the senior centers in Rowland Heights and Hacienda Heights.
Connie and Kailash Grover, Senior Club Pathfinders

Betty May she is not only a champion dancer, also excellent cook, she offer dance, cooking classes in community schools, she has unique skills, this "The Chinese Regional Gourmet Cookbook" book is her years of collection from her cooking classes. Food is an art in itself, her life with full of vitality, she love to share to everyone who enjoy to cook as much as love to dance.
Jeffrey Zhou, VOH

Betty has love for many, with sunshine personality, She love people, culture, music, art museum, is very arty person, she offer dance, flower arrangement , and cooking classes in community school, this cook book with beautiful photo and easy to follow recipe, you will love to own.
Cindy Chang, Real Estate Investor

My dearest friend Betty, she is a talented lady with fantastic cooking skills, she offers Chinese cooking and Italian cooking classes in community school. This authentic Chinese cook book has beautiful pictures and you will love the recipe.
Joyce Liu, VOH

In the cooking class
Betty May demonstration the pineapple prawns.

1 Timothy 6:8
If we have food and clothing. With these we shall be content.

CONTENTS

Ingredients Measurement Note: T – tablespoon, t – teaspoon, c – cup

"ANTS CLIMBING THE TREE"
螞蟻上樹
BEAN THREAD NOODLES WITH HOT BEAN PASTE (SZECHWAN)

INGREDIENTS:

2 packages bean threads
3 oz ground pork
1 T water
1 t cornstarch
1 T hot bean paste
1 t rice wine
1 T soy sauce
1 t sugar
1 t chopped ginger root
1 T chopped green onion
1-1/2 cups stock or water
1/4 t salt or to taste

PREPARATION:

Presoak 2 packages bean threads (transparent soy noodles) in warm water until soft. In a bowl, combine l t cornstarch and l T water and mix this into 3 oz ground pork. Preheat the wok, add 2 T canola oil, and bring to high heat. When hot, add l t chopped ginger root, 1T chopped green onion and stir-fry until the ginger is fragrant. Add the pork mixture to the wok and stir-fry until cooked through. Mix in 1 T hot bean paste, 1 t rice wine, 1 T soy sauce, and 1 t sugar. When heated through, add 1-1/2 cups stock or water and bring to a boil. Add 1/4 t salt or to taste. Add the softened bean threads and carefully cook uncovered stirring occasionally for about 8 min or until the stock is reduced and the noodles are almost dry and coated with the meat mixture. Serve immediately.

BAMBOO SHOOTS IN BROWN SAUCE

醬燒筍尖

STIR-FRIED SLENDER BAMBOO SHOOTS

INGREDIENTS:

3 cups slender bamboo shoots (fresh or canned)
2 T canola oil
1 T chopped Szechwan pickled mustard greens
2 green onions cut into 2 inch sections
2 T soy sauce
2 T water
1 T sweet bean paste
1 T oyster sauce
1 t rice wine
1/4 t sugar
1 t sesame oil
2 T water
1 t cornstarch

PREPARATION:

Blanch 3 cups slender bamboo shoots (fresh or canned). Heat the wok, add 2 T canola oil, and bring to high heat. Add 1 T chopped Szechwan pickled mustard greens and 2 green onions cut into 2-inch sections, stir-fry for 2 min. Add the bamboo shoots, 2 T soy sauce, 2 T water, 1 T sweet bean paste, 1 T oyster sauce, 1 t rice wine, a dash of sugar, and 1 t sesame oil stir-fry to mix well and cook for 5 min. In a separate bowl, combine 2 T water and 1 t cornstarch until dissolved. Add to the wok and stir until the sauce thickens. Remove from the wok, place on serving plate and serve.

BEEF AND ASPARAGUS
蘆筍牛柳
BEEF AND ASPARAGUS WITH CHINESE CROUTONS (CANTONESE)

INGREDIENTS:

4 oz beef tenderloin into
1/2 - inch cubes
1 t sweet bean paste
1 T rice wine
1 t soy sauce
3 T canola oil
1 green onion cut into 2-inch sections
1 piece white wood ear, presoaked and broken into small pieces
12 oz asparagus cut into

1-inch sections
1 Chinese crouton (yu tiao) cut into 1-inch sections
1 t soy sauce
1/4 t salt
1 T cornstarch
2 T water
1 t sesame oil
1 T chopped green onion for garnish

PREPARATION:

Cut 4oz beef tenderloin into 1/2-inch cubes. Place in a bowl and add 1 t sweet bean paste, 1 T rice wine, and 1 t soy sauce. Mix well and allow to marinate for 15 min at room temperature. Heat the wok, add 3 T canola oil and bring to high heat. Add the meat mixture and stir-fry until the meat colors. Remove with a slotted spoon or a wire skimmer and place in a sieve over a bowl to drain. Reheat the remaining oil and bring to high heat. Add 1 green onion cut into 2-inch sections. Stir-fry until fragrant. Add 1 cup dry white wood ear, presoaked and broken into small pieces, 12
oz fresh thin asparagus cut into 1-inch sections, and l Chinese crouton (yu tiao) cut into 1-inch sections. Stir-fry until well mixed. Add 1 t soy sauce, a dash of salt, and stir-fry until well mixed. In a separate bowl, combine 1 T cornstarch and 2 T water until dissolved. Add to the wok and stir-fry the mixture until the sauce thickens. Add a dash of sesame oil, sprinkle with 1 T chopped green onion and remove to a warm serving platter.

BUDDHA'S DELIGHT

羅漢齋

ANCIENT VEGETARIAN DISH (CANTONESE)

INGREDIENTS:

2 T canola oil
A few slice ginger root
2 piece green onion cut into 1-inch sections
2 cup presoak black mushrooms cut into half
2 cakes deep fried tofu (bean curd) cut in half
1 cup baby corn
1 cup presoaked white fungus broken into small pieces
1 cup precook (fried) gluten puffs

1 cup presoak lily flowers
2 t oyster sauce
1 T soy sauce
1 t sugar
1 T rice wine
1 T rice vinegar
1 cup water or stock
1/2 head Iceberg lettuce
1/2 cup snow peas

PREPAR ATION:

Heat the wok, add 2 T canola oil, bring to high heat, add a few slices ginger root, 2 green onions cut into 1-inch sections, and stir-fry until fragrant. Add a presoaked black mushrooms cut in half. Stir-fry until well mixed. Add 2 cakes deep fried tofu (bean curd) cut in half, 1 cup baby corn, 1 presoaked white fungus broken into small pieces, 1 cup precooked (fried) gluten puffs, and 1 cup presoaked tiger lily flowers. Stir-fry to mix well. Add 2 t oyster sauce, 1 T soy sauce, 1 t sugar, 1 T rice wine, 1 T rice vinegar, and 1 cup water or stock. Cook for 8 min over medium heat. In a

Chinese clay pot (sa guo), place 1/2 head Iceberg lettuce, pour the vegetable mixture over the lettuce and cook for 10 min over low heat. Add 1/2 cup snow peas and a few slices of carrot. Mix well and serve directly from the clay pot.

Note: For Buddhist monks, this dish can be cooked without ginger and green onion.

CHICKEN AND CORN SOUP

雞蓉玉米湯

MINCED CHICKEN AND SWEET CORN SOUP (CANTONESE)

INGREDIENTS:

5 oz ground chicken white meat
1 T rice wine
1/4 t salt
1 t cornstarch
One ear of fresh sweet yellow corn
4 cups chicken stock
2 T cornstarch
2 T water
1 egg white
1 T water
1 T pork sung* (fried ground pork powder)
White pepper powder

PREPARATION:

Place 5 oz ground chicken white meat in a bowl. Add 1 T rice wine, a dash of salt, and 1 t cornstarch, mix well and allow to marinate for 15 minutes at room temperature. Meanwhile, using a sharp knife, remove the kernels from one ear of fresh sweet yellow corn and set aside. Place 4 cups chicken stock in a large pot and bring to a boil. Add the corn and the chicken mixture, stirring to separate the chicken pieces. Bring to a boil and cook for 1 minute. Meanwhile, in a separate bowl, combine 2 T cornstarch and 2 T water until dissolved. Add to the soup and cook until thickened. In a Separate bowl, beat 1 egg white and 1 T water until just combined. Stirring the soup constantly, slowly pour the egg mixture into the hot soup so that it forms small ribbons. Garnish with pork sung* and serve in a heated bowl with white pepper powder on the side.

CHICKEN WITH PINE NUTS

松子雞粒

STIR-FRIED SHREDDED CHICKEN WITH PINE NUTS (CHEKIANG-KIANGSU)

INGREDIENTS:

12 oz chicken white meat
1 T rice wine
1 egg white
1 t cornstarch
1 T water
1/4 t salt
1/2 cup canola oil
1 t finely chopped ginger root
1 T finely chopped green onion
1/4 t white pepper powder
2 T water
2 t cornstarch
1/2 cup toasted pine nuts

PREPARATION:

Chop 12 oz chicken white meat into rice-size pieces and place in a bowl. Add 1 T rice wine, 1 egg white, 1 t cornstarch, 1 T water, and salt to taste. Mix well and let marinate for 15 min at room temperature. Heat the wok, add 1/2 cup canola oil, and bring to high heat. Add the chicken mixture and stir-fry stirring constantly until the meat changes color, about 2 min. Remove the meat with a slotted spoon or a wire skimmer and place it in a sieve set in a larger bowl to drain. Remove the oil, reheat the wok, and add 1 T of the reserved oil. Add 1 t finely

chopped ginger root, 1 T finely chopped green onion, and a dash of white pepper powder. Stir-fry until fragrant. Add the chicken and stir until heated through. In a separate bowl, combine 2 T water and 2 t cornstarch until dissolve. Add to the wok and stir until thickened. Remove to a serving plate, and sprinkle with 1/2 cup toasted pine nuts. Mix gently before serving.

CHINESE BROCCOLI
蠔油芥蘭
BROCCOLI WITH OYSTER SAUCE (CANTONESE)

INGREDIENTS:

3/4 lb Chinese broccoli (ji lan ci)
5-6 thin slices ginger root
6 cups water
1/2 t salt 1 T canola oil
2 T oyster sauce 1 T soy sauce 1 t sesame oil

PREPARATION:

Place 6 cups water in a stock pot or a large wok and add 5 to 6 thin slices of ginger root, 1/2 t salt or to taste, and 1 T canola oil and bring to a boil. Add 3/4 lb Chinese broccoli (ji lan ci) cut into 4 to 5-inch sections and cook for 3 min or until slightly softened. Remove the broccoli from the pot with a slotted spoon or a wire skimmer, drain, and place on a warm serving platter. In a separate bowl, mix 2 T oyster sauce, 1 T soy sauce, and dash of sugar. Pour the oyster sauce mixture over the broccoli. Add a dash of sesame oil and serve immediately.

"CLAMS IN THE CLOUDS"

蛤蜊蒸蛋

CLAMS STEAMED IN EGG CUSTARD (TAIWANESE)

INGREDIENTS:

10-12 pieces medium size live manila clams
3 slices of ginger root
3 eggs
2 T rice wine
1 t finely chopped garlic
1 t finely chopped ginger
1/4 t salt
1 t finely chopped green onions

PREPARATION:

Place 10-12 medium size fresh live Manila clams or cockles in the large bowl with filled with water. Allow the clams to sit in the water until the shells open slightly and they expel any sand they may contain. In a large pot, bring 5 cups of water to a boil. Add 3 slices of ginger root and the clams. Boil until the shells open completely. Remove with a slotted spoon or a wire skimmer, let drain, and set aside. In the bowl, combine 3 eggs with 2 T rice wine, 1 t finely chopped garlic, 1 t finely chopped ginger, a dash of salt, and 2 cup water. Stir well. Pour the egg mixture in to a shallow

glass or ceramic dish, about 2 inches deep. Place 4 cups of water in a steamer or a port large enough to hold the dish, place the dish in the steamer, cover and bring to a boil. Steam covered for 5 min over medium heat. Open the lid when the egg custard is slightly firm, add the clams evenly to the egg custard and continue to steam with the lid slightly ajar for 10 min over low heat. When the eggs are set, remove from the steamer and garnish with 1 t finely chopped green onion and serving directly from the dish.

CRAB OVER SWEET RICE

肉蟹糯米飯

STEAMED WHOLE CRAB OVER GLUTINOUS RICE (TAIWANESE)

INGREDIENTS:

2 to 2-1/4 lb live crab cut into 4-6 pieces
1 t salt
2 T rice wine
1-1/4 cups sweet rice
1-1/2 cups water
3 T canola oil
2 T presoaked and chopped dried shrimp
1 T chopped garlic
2 T dried scallion
1/2 cup presoaked and shredded black mushrooms
3 oz ground pork
2 T soy sauce
1/4 t sugar

PREPARATION:

Clean a 2 to 2-1/4 lb live crab and cut it into 4-6 pieces (or ask your butcher to clean and cut it for you, saving the top shell). Place crab pieces in the bowl and add 1 t salt, 2 T rice wine. Mix well and let marinate for 15 min at room temperature. Rinse 2 cups of sweet (glutinous) rice and place in a large pot, add 1-1/2 cups water, bring to a boil, and cook for about 3-4 min over high heat. Turn the heat to low and simmer for 6 min or until the rice is almost done. Heat the wok, add 3 T canola oil, and bring to high heat. Add 2 T presoaked and chopped dried shrimp, 1 T chopped garlic,

2 T dried scallion, and 1/2 cup presoaked and shredded black mushrooms. Stir-fry until fragrant. Add 3 oz ground pork and stir-fry until meat changes color. Add the precooked rice, 2 T soy sauce, a dash of sugar, and a dash of sesame oil. Stir-fry until evenly coated. Place on a serving platter, place the crab pieces on top of the sweet rice, and arrange shell on top of crab pieces. Place the platter in a steamer and steam for 25 min over low heat. Remove and serve.

CRISPY NOODLES WITH SEAFOOD

海鮮兩面黃

PAN-FRIED NOODLES WITH SHRIMP, SCALLOPS, AND SQUID (CANTONESE)

INGREDIENTS:

4 T canola oil
1 lb bundle of fresh egg wheat noodles
2 T canola oil
3 oz shelled and de-veined medium raw shrimp
3 oz bay scallops
3 oz of squid cut into 1-inch strips
1/4 t salt
1/4 black pepper powder
2 T canola oil
a few slices of ginger root
2 green onions cut into 1-inch sections

a few slices of carrot
1 cup shredded Chinese cabbage
a few stems Chinese broccoli
2 cups chicken stock
1/4 t black pepper powder
1 T oyster sauce
1 t hoisin sauce
1/4 t salt
1/4 t sugar
3 T water
2 T cornstarch

PREPARATION:

In a non-stick pan large enough to hold the noodles, add 4 T canola oil and raise the heat to medium-high. Gently fluff a 1 lb bundle of fresh egg wheat noodles to separate them. When the pan is hot, add the noodles and saute until browned and crispy (the noodles should still be soft inside the bundle) dusting them occasionally with water flicked from the fingertips to keep the noodles moist. When browned, turn the noodles over and repeat. Set aside to a serving platter and keep warm. To the wok, add 2 T canola oil and bring to high heat. When hot, add 3 oz raw shelled and de-veined medium shrimp, 3 oz bay scallops, 3 oz of squid cut into 1-inch strips, 1/4 t salt or to taste, and 1/4 black pepper powder. Stir-fry until the shrimp turn pink and scallops and squid turn white. Remove the seafood from the wok and set aside. In a bowl, mix 3 T water and 2 T cornstarch until dissolved. To the wok, add 2 T canola oil, a few slices of ginger root, and 2 green onions cut into 1-inch sections. Stir-fry until fragrant. Add a few slices of carrot, 1 cup shredded Chinese cabbage, and a few stems Chinese broccoli. Stir-fry until the vegetables are very slightly softened. Add 2 cups chicken stock, a dash of black pepper powder, 1 T oyster sauce, 1 t hoisin sauce, a dash of salt or to taste, and a dash of sugar. Bring to a boil. Add the seafood. Add the cornstarch mixture to the wok and cook quickly until thickened. Pour the seafood mixture over the crispy noodles and mix slightly just before serving.

DRY SAUTÉED STRING BEANS

乾扁四季豆

STRING BEANS WITH GROUND PORK (SZECHWAN)

INGREDIENTS:

1 lb Chinese string beans
3 oz ground pork
2 T presoaked and chopped dried shrimp
1 t chopped green or red chili pepper
2 oz chopped pickled mustard green
1 T soy sauce
1 t water
¼ t sugar
1 T chopped green onion

PREPARATION:

Remove any vein string from 1 lb Chinese string beans, cut into about 3-inch sections, rinse and dry. Heat the wok, add 1/2 cup canola oil, and bring to high heat. Before putting the string beans in the wok, turn off the heat (to prevent the oil from spattering). Add the string beans, raise the heat and stir-fry on medium heat until just softened. Remove the string beans with a slotted spoon or a wire skimmer. Remove the oil from the wok. Return 1 T of the reserved oil and reheat it. Stir-fry 3 oz ground pork until the meat is cooked through and is broken up. Add 2

T presoaked and chopped dried shrimp, 1 t chopped green or red chili pepper and 2 oz chopped pickled mustard greens. Return the beans to the wok; add 1 T soy sauce, 1 t water, and a dash of sugar. Stir quickly over high heat for a few seconds (the string beans should not be overcooked but still crunchy). Sprinkle with 1 T chopped green onion and a dash of sesame oil. Serve immediately.

EGGPLANT WITH MISO PASTE

味噌茄子

SAUTÉED EGGPLANT (TAIWANESE)

INGREDIENTS:

4 medium Oriental eggplants
2 T canola oil
1 T sliced garlic
1 green onion cut into 1-inch sections
1 t miso paste
1 t water
1 t soy sauce
1/4 t sugar

PREPARATION:

Wash and remove the ends from 4 medium Oriental eggplants and cut into 3-inch sections. Cut each section into quarters. Heat the wok, add 2 T canola oil, and bring to high heat. Add 1 T sliced garlic and stir-fry until fragrant. Add the eggplant and sauté over the low heat for 15 min, stirring occasionally, until the eggplant is soft and cooked through. Add 1 green onion cut into 1-inch sections, mix well. In a bowl, combine 1 t miso paste, 1 t water, 1 t soy sauce, and 1/4 t sugar, mix well. Add sauce mixture to the cooked eggplant and stir. Remove to warm plate and serve.

"EIGHT TREASURES" RICE PUDDING

八寶飯

EIGHT RICE PUDDING WITH RED BEAN PASTE

INGREDIENTS:

2 cups precooked sweet rice
1 slice pineapple
1/2 cup sweet kidney beans
1/4 cup raisins
1/4 cup dried red dates
1/4 cup candied fruit
1 T canola oil   2 T sugar
1/2 cup red bean paste
1 cup pineapple juice
1 T water   1 T cornstarch

PREPARATION:

Place a slice of canned pineapple, drained and patted dry with a paper towel, in the center of a 2 to 3-inch high, oiled medium size glass or ceramic bowl or dish. Around the pineapple, arrange 1/2 cup sweet kidney beans, 1/4 cup raisins, a few pieces of presoak dry red dates, and a few pieces candied fruit in a decorative symmetrical or abstract pattern. Place 2 cups precooked sweet (glutinous) rice and add 1 T canola oil and 2 T sugar, mix will. Take 1/2 of the rice mixture and carefully place it on top of the fruit arrangement. Spread 1/2 cup red bean paste over the rice mixture and then add the remaining rice mixture spreading to

cover the red bean paste (to form three layers). Place the bowl in a steamer and steam over medium heat for 45 min. In a small saucepan, bring to boil 1 cup pineapple juice. In a separate bowl, combine 2 T water and 1 T cornstarch until dissolved. Add this to the pineapple juice and cook until it thickens. Remove the bowl containing the rice from the steamer and de-mold it by carefully inverting it onto a warm serving platter. Pour the pineapple glaze over the rice pudding.

GLAZED WALNUT SHRIMP
蜜汁核桃蝦
DEEP-FRIED SHRIMP WITH GLAZED WALNUTS (CANTONESE)

INGREDIENTS:

12-16 raw large shrimp
1 t salt
1 t baking soda
1 egg white
1 t canola oil
2 t cornstarch
1 T flour
1 cup canola oil
3 T Chinese mayonnaise
2 cups shredded lettuce
1/2 cup glazed walnuts

PREPARATION:

Remove the shells, legs, and veins from 12-16 raw large shrimp. Condition the shrimp by adding 1 t salt and 1 t baking soda, stir* for a few minutes, rinse and pat dry with a paper towel. Add 1 egg white, 1 t canola oil, 2 t cornstarch, 1 T flour, and a dash of salt, stir until the shrimp are coated. Heat the wok; add 1 cup canola oil (or enough to cover the shrimp). Add the shrimp and deep fry until the shrimp change color to pink. Remove the shrimp with a slotted spoon or a wire skimmer and place them in a sieve set in a large bowl to drain or on paper towel to drain.

Place the shrimp in a bowl, add 3 T Chinese mayonnaise and toss until coated. Place the shrimp on 2 cups shredded lettuce, top the shrimp with 1/2 cup glazed walnuts, and serve immediately.

* Alternately gently rub or massage the mixture into the shrimp with the palm of the hand.

GOLDEN CHICKEN ROLLS

黃金雞捲

CHICKEN WRAPPED IN BEAN CURD SHEET (TAIWANESE)

INGREDIENTS:

8 oz fish paste
4 oz ground chicken
1/2 cup chopped brown onion
1/2 cup chopped carrot
2 T chopped water chestnut (or bamboo shoots)
2 T chopped green onion
1 T hoisin sauce
1 T ketchup
1 t soy sauce

2 T cornstarch
1 T rice wine
1/4 t salt
1 t sugar
1 t sesame oil
¼ t black pepper powder
2 T water
1 T flour
1 large bean curd sheet*
2 cups canola oil for frying

PREPARATION:

Place 8 oz fish paste and 4 oz ground chicken in a bowl. Add 1/2 cup chopped brown onion, 1/2 cup chopped carrot, 2 T chopped water chestnut (or bamboo shoots), and 2 T chopped green onion. Mix well. Add 2 T cornstarch, 1 T rice wine, 1 t sugar, 1 t sesame oil, a dash of salt, and a dash of black pepper powder. Mix well. In a separate bowl, combine 1 T hoisin sauce, 1 T ketchup, and 1 t soy sauce for the dipping sauce. In a separate bowl, combine 2 T water and 1 T flour until well mixed. Place 1 large bean curd sheet* on a cutting board and cut into six 8-inch

by 10-inch pieces and set aside. Place a bamboo mat slightly larger than the sheets on the cutting board. Place one bean curd sheet on the bamboo mat and place 1/6 of the mixture on the bean curd sheet in ribbon along the long edge. Using the bamboo mat, roll up the bean curd sheet. Seal the roll by applying the flour mixture along the long edge of the bean curd sheet. Pinch the ends closed. Repeat for each of the five remaining bean curd sheets. Heat the wok, add 2 cups canola oil and bring to high heat. Slide two chicken rolls into the oil, lower the heat to medium and deep-fry turning occasionally until even golden brown. Remove with a slotted spoon or a wire whisk and place on paper towels to drain. Repeat for the remaining rolls, Cut the rolls diagonally into six pieces and arrange on a warm serving platter. Serve with the hoisin sauce mixture for dipping.

Note * Bean curd sheets come in a package contain a single large folded circular sheet about 2 feet across or sometimes in a stack of large precut sheet.

35

GOLDEN POT STICKERS

鍋貼

PAN FRIED DUMPLINGS (CANTONESE)

INGREDIENTS:

8 oz ground pork or chicken
8 oz chopped raw shelled shrimp
1 T soy sauce
1 t sugar
1/2 t salt
1/4 t black pepper powder
1 T sesame oil
2 T cornstarch
1 T chopped ginger root
2 T chopped green onion
1 cup chopped bamboo shoots

1 T rice wine
4 T water
1 T flour
2 T chili sauce
1 T rice vinegar
1 T soy sauce
1 T sesame oil
1/2 cup water
1 T rice vinegar
1 t canola oil

PREPARATION:

Place 8 oz ground pork or chicken in a bowl and add 8 oz chopped raw shelled shrimp, mix well. Add 1 T soy sauce, 1 t sugar, 1/2 t salt or to taste, 1/4 t black pepper powder, 1 T sesame oil, 2 T cornstarch, mix well. Add 1 T chopped ginger root, 2 T chopped green onion, 1 cup chopped bamboo shoots, and 1 T rice wine, mix well and set aside. In a separate bowl, combine 4 T water with 1 T flour. In a bowl, combine 2 T chili sauce, 1 T rice vinegar, 1 T soy sauce, and 1 T sesame oil for the dipping sauce. Open one package of pot sticker (guo tie) skins, and place one skin on a

cutting board. Place 1 T of the meat/shrimp mixture in the center. Draw a strip along one edge with the water/flour mixture and fold the dumpling in half pressing the edges closed but being careful to leave both ends open. Repeat until the meat mixture is used up, making about 25 dumplings. In a separate bowl, combine 1/2 cup water with 1 T rice vinegar. Heat a non-stick wok and add 1 t canola oil and swirl to coat. When hot, picking up the dumpling carefully by the closed edge, place two rows of eight dumplings in the wok. Sauté for 2 minutes then sprinkle with 2 T of the water/vinegar mixture. Turn heat to medium and over. Cook for another minute until the liquid has been absorbed. Sprinkle again and cook covered until the liquid is absorbed. Repeat until the dumpling skins are cooked through (usually two or three cycles). Remove the cover and sauté until the bottoms of the dumplings are golden brown and slightly crisp. Remove and repeat for the remaining dumplings. Arrange on a serving platter, brown side up. Serve the dipping sauce on the side.

"GOOD LUCK" PORK CUTLETS
吉利肉排

BREADED PORK LOIN (CANTONESE)

INGREDIENTS:

2/3 lb pork loin
1 t rice wine
1 t sugar
1/4 t black pepper powder
1/4 t five spice powder
1/4 t salt
1/2 cup cornstarch
1 beaten egg
1 cup breadcrumbs
1 cup canola oil for frying
cilantro for garnish
spicy salt

PREPARATION:

Cut 2/3 lb pork loin into 1/2-inch slices. Tenderize the meat slices by placing one slice in a plastic bag and gently pounding it with a rubber mallet until it has doubled in size. (The plastic bag prevents the thin meat slices from sticking to the cutting board.) Repeat for the rest of the meat slices. Place the tenderized meat slices in a bowl and add 1 t rice wine, 1 t sugar, 1/4 black pepper powder, 1/4 t five spice powder, 1/4 t salt, mix well. Let marinate at room temperature for 15 min. Place 1/2 cup cornstarch on a plate. Place 1 beaten egg on a second plate or in a shallow
bowl, and 1 cup breadcrumbs in a third. Place a meat slice in cornstarch and turn it over making sure both sides are well dusted. Then place in the beaten egg, again covering both sides. And then place it in the breadcrumbs, pressing gently, until it is well coated. Heat the wok, add 1 cup canola oil, and bring to high the heat. Carefully slide one slice into the hot oil and deep-fry for 30 sec. Turn the meat over, continue to fry over medium heat for 20 sec or until evenly golden. Remove the meat and drain, pat dry with paper towel, and then cut the meat into 2-inch sections. Repeat the breading and frying for the remaining meat slices. Place in warm serving plate and garnish with cilantro. Serve with spicy salt on the side.

GREEN ONION AND EGG CREPE

蛋餅

CHINESE BREAKFAST CREPE (TAIWANESE)

INGREDIENTS:

2 eggs
4 T all purpose flour
3/4 cup water
1 t sesame oil
4 T canola oil
1/4 t salt or to taste
2 T chopped green onion

PREPARATION:

Sift 4 T all purpose flour into a medium bowl. Add 3/4 cup water, mix well. Add 2 eggs and beat them into the flour mixture. Add 1 t sesame oil, 1/4 t salt or to taste. Add 2 T chopped green onion. Mix well until smooth (do not use an electric mixer or blender). Heat a flat pan, coat thoroughly with 1 T canola oil (the amount of oil can be reduced if you use a non-stick pan). Turn the heat off, pour 1/2 cup of the crepe mixture onto the hot pan and rock the pan gently to spread the mixture evenly to make a 7-inch crepe. Raise heat to medium. Cook for 2 to 3 min

until the bottom of the crepe has light brown spots. Turn and cook the other side for 1 to 2 min until the crepe is cooked through. Repeat, adding enough oil to the pan so the crepe won't stick, until the mixture is used up. Makes 4 crepes, about 7-inches in diameter. Serve the crepes flat or rolled.

HAND CUT RICE NOODLES
炒牛河

STIR-FRIED HO FEN NOODLE SHEETS WITH BEEF (CANTONESE)

INGREDIENTS:

1 lb rice noodles sheets
6 cups water
6 oz flank steak
1 t rice wine
1 T water
1 t cornstarch
1/4 t salt
4 T canola oil

5 thin slices ginger root
2 green onions cut into
1-inch sections
3 T soy sauce
1 cup stock
1/4 t black pepper powder
1 cup bean sprouts cilantro sprigs for garnish

PREPARATION:

Cut 6 oz flank steak into thin 2-inch by 4-inch slices. Place the meat in a bowl and add 1 t rice wine, 1 T water, 1 t cornstarch, and 1/4 t salt to taste. Mix until the meat is coated and let marinate for 15 min at room temperature. Cut 1 lb rice noodles sheets into 1-inch wide strips (or any other size or shape desired). Place 6 cups water in a large pot and bring to a boil. Add the noodle strips and stir briskly for 15 sec to loosen the noodles. Remove the noodles with a sieve and refresh them by placing the sieve in a large pot or bowl of cold water and shaking the noodles. When cool, about 1 min, remove and

place in a bowl. Add 1 T canola oil and mix to prevent the noodles from sticking. Heat the wok, add 4 T canola oil and bring to high heat. Add the meat mixture and stir-fry until meat changes color and is cooked through. Remove the meat with a slotted spoon or a wire skimmer and place it in a sieve set over a larger bowl or on paper towels to drain. Reheat the remaining oil and add 5 thin slices ginger root, 2 green onions cut into 1-inch sections, and stir-fry until fragrant. Add 3 T soy sauce, 1 cup stock, 1/4 t black pepper powder. Bring the sauce to a boil. Add the precooked rice noodles strips, 1 cup bean sprouts, and mix well. Add the meat, and mix for a few seconds until heated through. Transfer to warm platter, garnish with cilantro sprigs and serve.

HOT AND SOUR SOUP
酸辣湯
HOT AND SOUR SOUP (BEIJING)

INGREDIENTS:

1/3 cups shredded baked or firm tofu (bean curd)
1/3 cups shredded presoaked wood ears
1/3 cups shredded presoaked black mushroom
1/3 cups shredded presoaked bamboo shoot
1/3 cups lily flowers presoaked and knotted
3 oz shredded pork loin or chicken
1 T soy sauce
1 t cornstarch
1 t sesame oil
6 cups water or stock

2 T soy sauce
4 T rice vinegar
1 t rice wine
1/4 t salt
1 t sugar
2 t black pepper powder
1 T sesame oil
2 T shredded green onion
2 T shredded ginger root
3 T water
3 T cornstarch
2 eggs, beaten

PREPARATION:

Place 3 oz shredded pork loin or chicken in a mixing bowl and add 1 T soy sauce, 1 t cornstarch, 1 t sesame oil. Mix until coated and let marinate for 10 min at room temperature. In a separate bowl, beat 2 eggs with a dash of salt and 1 t rice wine. In a stockpot, bring to boil 6 ups water and add 1/3 cups shredded baked or firm tofu (bean curd), 1/3 cups shredded presoaked wood ears, 1/3 cups shredded presoaked black mushroom, 1/3 cups shredded presoaked bamboo shoot, 1/3 cups presoaked and knotted lily flowers. Bring to boil again. Add the meat mixture and

stir to separate. Stir in 2 T soy sauce, 4 T rice vinegar, 1 t sugar, and a dash of salt. Slowly add the beaten egg mixture in a thin stream, stirring gently. In a separate bowl, mix 3 T water and 3 T cornstarch until dissolved and add the mixture to the soup, cooking until it thickens. Then add 2 T shredded ginger root, 2 T shredded green onion, 2 t black pepper powder, and 1 T sesame oil. Place in large soup bowl or tureen.

HUNAN LAMB

湖南羊肉

SPICY LAMB WITH LEEKS (HUNAN)

INGREDIENTS:

12 oz of thinly sliced lamb
1 t finely chopped garlic
1 T soy sauce
1 T rice wine
1/2 t sugar
1/2 cup canola oil
2 T thinly sliced garlic
2 T chopped green onion
1 t chopped hot chili pepper
1 T fermented black beans
2 t hot bean paste
1 T soy sauce
1 leek cut diagonally into 1 inch sections
Cilantro sprigs for garnish

PREPARATION:

Place 12 oz of thinly sliced lamb in a bowl. Add 1t finely chopped garlic, 1 T soy sauce, 1 T rice wine, 2 t hot bean paste, and 1/2 sugar. Mix well and let marinate for 15 min at room temperature. Heat the wok, add 1/2 cup canola oil, and bring to high heat. Add the lam mixture and fry until cooked through, about 1 min. remove the meat with a slotted spoon or a wire skimmer and place it in a sieve set over a larger bowl to drain. Remove the oil from the wok and return 1 T of the reserved oil. Reheat the wok, add 2 T thinly sliced garlic, 2 T chopped green onion, 1 t chopped hot chili  pepper, 1 T fermented black beans, and stir-fry until fragrant. Add 1 leek cut diagonally into 1 inch sections and stir for a few seconds until the leek is heated through and slightly softened. Add 1 T soy sauce, mix well, remove to serving plate, garnish with cilantro.

"JIN-DU" PORK CHOPS
京都肉排
SWEET AND SOUR PORK CHOPS (MANDARIN STYLE)

INGREDIENTS :

1-1/2 lb thin pork chops
1 t rice wine
1 T soy sauce
1 t sugar
1 T chopped garlic
2 T cornstarch
1/4 t salt
1 cup canola oil

1/2 cup shredded brown onion
3 T ketchup
1 T dark vinegar
2 T water
1 t sugar
1 t hot sesame oil
A few pieces of shredded onion

PREPARATION:

Place 1-1/2 lb thin pork chops in a shallow bowl and add 1 t rice wine, 1 T soy sauce, 1 t sugar, 1 T chopped garlic, 2 T cornstarch and a dash of salt. Mix until the meat is coated and let marinate for 15 min at room temperature. Heat the wok and add 1 cup canola oil (or enough to cover the pork chops). Deep-fry the chops until meat changes color and is cooked through. Remove the meat with a slotted spoon or a wire skimmer and place in a sieve set over a larger bowl or on paper towels to drain. Remove the oil from the wok and return 2 T of the reserved oil. Reheat

the wok, add 1/2 cup shredded brown onion, stir-fry for 30 sec. Add 3 T ketchup, 1 T dark vinegar, 2 T water, and 1 t sugar, stir the sauce for 10 sec. Add the chops to the sauce mixture, stir until coated. Add 1 t hot sesame oil, stir for a few seconds until just heated through. Remove to warm serving platter and garnish with shredded onion.

"KUNG PAO" CHICKEN

宮保雞丁

SPICY CHICKEN WITH PEANUTS (SZECHWAN)

INGREDIENTS:

1 lb chicken meat
1/2 cup dried red chili peppers
1 T chopped onion
1/2 cu peanuts
1/2 cup canola oil for frying
1 T soy sauce
1 t rice wine
2 t cornstarch

1 T soy sauce
1 t rice wine
1 t dark vinegar
1 t sugar
1 t sesame oil
3 T water
1 T cornstarch

PREPARATION:

Cut 1 lb chicken white meat into bite-sized pieces and place in a mixing bowl. Add 1 T soy sauce, 1 t rice wine, 2 t cornstarch. Stir until coated and let marinate for 15 min at room temperature. Add 1 T canola oil to the chicken mixture and stir to coat the pieces (so they won't stick together in the wok). To the wok, add 1/2 cup canola oil (or enough to cover the chicken) and bring to high heat. When hot, add the chicken pieces and deep-fry until the meat turns white. Remove the chicken with a slotted spoon or a wire skimmer place it in a sieve set in a larger bowl. Remove the oil from the wok and return 1 T of the reserved oil and reheat it. Stir-fry 1/2 cup halved hot red chili peppers on low heat until fragrant. (For less spice, use whole peppers rather than halves.) Return the chicken to the wok and add 1 T soy sauce, 1 t rice wine, 1 t dark vinegar, 1 t sugar, and mix well. In a Small bowl, mix 3 T water and 1 T cornstarch until dissolved and add to the chicken mixture. Stir-fry quickly until the sauce thickens. Add 1/2 cup whole roasted peanuts, 1 T chopped onion, and a dash of sesame oil. Serve immediately with white rice.

"LIONS HEAD" CASSEROLE

砂鍋獅子頭

CABBAGE-WRAPPED MEATBALL CASSEROLE (SHANGHAI)

INGREDIENTS:

1 lb ground pork
1 T rice wine
1/4 salt
1/4 black pepper powder
1 T chopped green onion
1 t chopped ginger root
1 egg
1 T soy sauce
2 T water

2 T canola oil
2 thin slices ginger root
1 green onion cut into
1-inch sections
1 lb Chinese cabbage (san
dong bai cai)
4 T cornstarch
2 T soy sauce
2 T water

1 cup canola oil for frying
2 cups water or chicken
stock
1 T cornstarch
2 T water
1 t sesame oil cilantro
springs for garnish

PREPARATION:

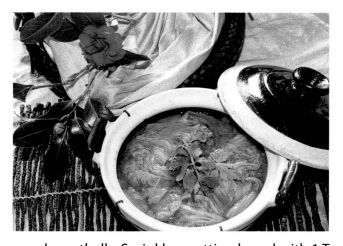

In a bowl, combine 1 lb ground pork, 1 T rice wine, a dash of salt, a dash of black pepper powder, 1 T chopped green onion, and 1 t chopped ginger root. Add 1 egg, 1 T soy sauce, 2 T water, beat by hand for one minute until smooth (extended beating insures light meatballs). Refrigerate for 15 min until the mixture of firm. In a Chinese ceramic casserole (sa guo) place a 2 T canola oil, 2 thin slices ginger root, 1 green onion cut into 1-inch sections, and stir-fry until fragrant. Add 1 lb Chinese cabbage (san dong bai cai)cut into 2-inch sections (reserving 2 whole leaves), and stir-fry quickly. Divide the meat mixture into four equal meatballs. Sprinkle a cutting board with 1 T cornstarch. In a separate dish, combine 2 T soy sauce and 2 T water. Heat the wok, add 1 cup canola oil (or enough to cover the meat balls), and bring to high heat. Roll one meatball through the cornstarch until evenly coated. Dip in the soy sauce mixture until evenly coated and put it in the hot oil. Quickly repeat the coating the other three meatballs. Deep fry for about 2 minutes until the outside is golden brown (they will be cooked further). Remove the meatballs with a slotted spoon or a wire skimmer and place in a sieve over a large bowl to drain. To the casserole, add 2 cups water or chicken stock, and bring to a boil. Add the meatballs and cover with several whole leaves of Chinese cabbage. Cover, lower the heat, and simmer for 30 minutes or until the meatballs are cooked through and the cabbage is soft. In a separate bowl, mix 1 T cornstarch and 2 T water until dissolved. Add to the casserole and continue simmering until thickened. Add a dash of sesame oil and garnish with cilantro sprigs. Serve directly from the sa guo.

LOTUS ROOT SALAD

涼拌蓮藕

MARINATED LOTUS ROOT (BEIJING)

INGREDIENTS:

2 sections fresh lotus root
6 cups water
2 T rice vinegar
1 T sugar
1/4 t salt
1 t oyster sauce
1 t chopped green onion
1/4 t sesame oil
1 red chili pepper thinly sliced

PREPARATION:

Rinse and peel 2 sections fresh lotus root and slice thinly. In a large pot, bring 6 cups water and 1 T rice vinegar to a boil and cook the slices for 5 min. or until slightly softened but still crispy. Remove and refresh in cold water, then drain. Place in a bowl and add 1 T rice vinegar, 1 T sugar, 1/4 t salt, 1 t oyster sauce, and 1 t chopped green onion. Mix until coated and let marinate for an hour at room temperature. Transfer to serving platter and garnish with thinly sliced red chili pepper and serve.

"MA-PO'S" TOFU

麻婆豆腐

SPICY BEAN CURD (SZECHWAN)

INGREDIENTS:

1 (19 oz) package soft bean curd (tofu)
3 oz ground pork
3 T canola oil
1 T hot bean paste
1 t chopped ginger root
1 t chopped garlic
1 T chopped green onion
1 T soy sauce

1 T rice wine
3/4 cup water
1/4 t salt
1/4 peppercorn powder
1/4 t sesame oil
2 T water
1 T cornstarch
2 T chopped green onion

PREPARATION:

Cut one (19 oz) package soft bean curd (tofu) into bite size cubes and set aside. Heat the wok, add 3 T canola oil and bring to high heat. Add 1 t chopped ginger root, 1 T chopped green onion and 1 t chopped garlic, and stir-fry until fragrant. Add 3 oz ground pork and 1 T hot bean paste (two tablespoons for a spicier dish), stir-fry until the meat is cooked through. Add 1 T rice wine, 3/4 cup water or stock, 1 T soy sauce, 1/4 t salt or to taste. When the sauce comes to a boil, add the tofu cubes and cook for 5 min over medium heat. Meanwhile, in a separate bowl,

mix 1 T cornstarch and 2 T water until dissolved. Add to the tofu mixture and cook until the mixture thickens stirring gently to avoid breaking up the tofu into too small pieces. Add a dash of peppercorn powder and a dash of sesame oil. Transfer to a heated shallow bowl. Garnish with 2 T chopped green onion and serve immediately.

Note: Ma Po translates literally as "Pock-marked face mother."

MINCED QUAIL IN LETTUCE CUPS

生菜鴿鬆

LETTUCE-WRAPPED QUAIL AND CHICKEN LIVER (CANTONESE)

INGREDIENTS:

1 medium head iceberg lettuce
3 T hoisin sauce
1 T sweet bean paste
1 quail (about 6 oz)
4 oz ground pork
3 parboiled and finely chopped chicken livers
1 T oyster sauce
1/4 t suga
1 t sesame oil
2 T water
1 t cornstarch
3 T canola oil
1 T chopped garlic

1 T chopped green onion
1/4 t salt
1 T finely chopped ginger
2 T finely chopped bamboo shoots
2 T finely chopped water chestnut
2 T chopped asparagus
1 T presoaked and finely chopped black mushroom
1 T rice wine
2 T canola oil
1 cooked and finely chopped egg yolk
1/4 t black pepper powder

PREPARATION:

To prepare the lettuce cups: Take one medium head of iceberg lettuce and carefully peel off the individual leaves rinsing if necessary. Stack about 12 lettuce cups on a plate. To prepare the sauce: In a small bowl, mix 3 T hoisin sauce with 1 T sweet bean paste. To prepare the filling: Remove the meat from one quail (about 6oz), chop finely. Place the quail meat into a mixing bowl, add 4 oz ground pork, 3 parboiled and finely chopped chicken livers, 1 T oyster sauce, a dash of sugar, 1 t sesame oil, 2 T water, 1 t cornstarch, and mix thoroughly. Place 3 T

canola oil in the wok and raise to high heat. Add 1 T chopped garlic, 1 T chopped green onion, salt to taste, 1 T finely chopped ginger, and stir-fry until fragrant. Add 2 T finely chopped bamboo shoots, 2 T finely chopped water chestnut, 2 T chopped asparagus, 1 T presoaked and finely chopped black mushroom, and 1 T rice wine. Stir-fry until well mixed. Remove from wok with a slotted spoon or a wire skimmer and set aside. Add 2 T canola oil to the wok and raise to high heat. When hot, add the meat mixture and stir-fry until cooked through, about 30 sec. Stir in 1 cooked and finely chopped egg yolk and a dash of black pepper powder. Return the vegetable mixture to the wok and mix quickly until combined and heated through. Place on warmed serving dish and serve with lettuce cups and a small dish of the hoisin sauce. Allow each person to assemble the dish by placing about 1/2 t of the sauce in the bottom of a lettuce cup and filling it with about 2 T of the meat/vegetable mixture. This dish is eaten with the hands.

MONGOLIAN BEEF

蔥爆牛肉

STIR-FRIED TENDERLOIN WITH GREEN ONION (MONGOLIA)

INGREDIENTS:

1 lb top sirloin steak or tenderloin
1 T soy sauce
1 T rice wine
1 t sugar
1 T cornstarch
3 green onion cut into 2 inch sections
1/2 cup slices bamboo shoots
2 T soy sauce
1 t sugar
1/4 t black pepper powder
2 T water
1 t cornstarch
1 t sesame oil

PREPARATION:

Slice 1 lb top sirloin steak or tenderloin into thin ribbons. Add 1 T soy sauce, 1 T rice wine, 1 t sugar, 1 T cornstarch, stir to coat and let marinate for 15 min at room temperature. Heat the wok, add 1/2 cup canola oil or enough cover the beef pieces, and bring to high heat. Fry the meat for 3 min or until the meat is cooked through. Remove the meat with a slotted spoon or a wire skimmer and place it in a sieve set in a larger bowl or on paper towels to drain. Remove the oil from the wok and return 2 T of the reserved oil to the wok. Reheat the wok, add 3 green onions cut into 2-inch
sections, and 1/2 cup slices bamboo shoots, stir-fry for 30 sec. Add the meat , 2 T soy sauce, 1 t sugar and a dash of black pepper powder, mix well. In a separate bowl, mix 2 T water and 1 t cornstarch until dissolved, add to the beef mixture. Stir-fry for 30 sec. or until the sauce thickens. Add dash sesame oil and serve immediately.

PINEAPPLE PRAWNS

果律蝦球

DEEP FRIED PRAWNS WITH PINEAPPLE

INGREDIENTS:

3/4 lb jumbo raw shrimp
1 t salt
1 t baking soda
1/4 t salt or to taste
1 egg white
2 t cornstarch
1 T canola oil

1 cup canola oil
1/2 cup diced fresh pineapple
2 T Chinese mayonnaise
A pineapple cut in a bowl or basket shape (optional)
1 t sesame seeds

PREPARATION:

Remove the shells, veins and legs from 3/4 lb jumbo raw prawns (or shrimp). Condition the prawns by adding 1 t salt and 1 t baking soda, stir* for a few minutes, rinse and pat dry with a paper towel. Place the prawns in a bowl and add 1/4 t salt or to taste, 1 egg white, and 2 t cornstarch. Mix well until coated and refrigerate for 15 min. Remove from refrigerator and add 1 T canola oil to prawns mixture, mix until coated. Heat the wok, add 1 cup canola oil and bring to high heat. Reduce heat before adding the prawns (to prevent the oil from spattering), add the prawns and raise the heat. Deep-fry over the high heat for 2-3 min or until the prawns turn pink, stirring gently to separate them. Remove with s slotted spoon or a sieve-ladle and place them in a sieve set in a larger bowl or on paper towels to drain and then place in a bowl. Remove all the oil from the wok and add 1/2 cup dice fresh pineapple, a dash of salt, and stir-fry for 2 min. Remove from the wok and add to the prawns. Add 2 T Chinese mayonnaise, toss until coated. Place on a warm serving platter, or place in a pineapple cut in a bowl or basket shape. Sprinkle with 1 t sesame seeds as garnish, and serve immediately.

* Alternately gently rub or massage the mixture into the prawns with the palm of the hand.
A pineapple cut in a bowl or basket shape (optional)

PORK CROQUETTE SOUP

粉絲肉丸湯

CROQUETTE WITH BEAN THREAD AND CUCUMBER SOUP

INGREDIENTS:

8 oz ground pork
3 oz bean thread noodles
1 t chopped ginger root
1 T chopped green onion
1/2 t salt or to taste
2 T soy sauce
2 T cornstarch
1 T rice wine
1 egg white

5 cups stock or water
Several slices Szechwan pickled mustard green
Several slices cucumber
Several slices tomato
1 T chopped Chinese celery
1/2 t white pepper powder
1 t sesame oil

PREPARATION:

Place 5 cups stock or water into a stockpot, bring to a boil. Add a few slices of Szechwan pickled mustard greens. Place 8 oz ground pork in the bowl, add 1 t chopped ginger root, 1 T chopped green onion, 2 T soy sauce, 1 T rice wine, 2 T cornstarch, 1 egg white and salt to taste. Mix well. Wet a soup-spoon (about 1 T in size), scoop out heaping portions of the meat mixture, and drop gently into the boiling liquid. Cook for 15 min or until the croquettes rise to the surface. Add 3 oz presoaked bean thread noodles. Cook for 3 min. Add a dash of white pepper powder and a dash

of sesame oil. Just before serving, add a few thin slices of tomato, a few thin slices of cucumber, and 1 T chopped Chinese celery as garnish.

PORK LOIN WITH PICKLED CUCUMBER

花瓜肉絲

HOME STYLE

INGREDIENTS:

3/4 lb pork loin
1 T soy sauce
1 t rice wine
2 T water
2 t cornstarch
1/2 cup canola oil
3 green onions cut into 1-inch sections
1/2 cup shredded pickled cucumber
3 T juice from the pickled cucumbers

PREPARATION:

Shred 3/4 lb pork loin to matchstick-size pieces. Add 1 T soy sauce, 1 t rice wine, 2 T water, and 2 t cornstarch. Mix until coated, marinate at room temperature for 15 min. Heat the wok, add 1/2 cup canola oil and bring to high heat. Add the shredded pork mixture and fry until the meat changes color. Remove the meat with a slotted spoon or a wire skimmer and place it in a sieve set over a larger bowl to drain. Remove the oil from the wok and return 1 T of the reserved oil. Reheat the wok and add 3 green onions cut into 1-inch sections, stir-fry until fragrant. Add 1/2 cup

shredded pickled cucumber. Stir-fry for 30 sec. Remove to serving plate and serve immediately.

PRAWNS WITH CUCUMBER

小黃瓜炒蝦球

STIR-FRIED PRAWNS WITH CUCUMBER

INGREDIENTS:

12 large raw prawns (or shrimp)
2 T rice wine
2 T cornstarch
1/4 t salt
3 T cup canola oil
1 t chopped ginger root
1 T chopped green onion
2 T chopped presoaked wood ears
1 sliced Chinese cucumber
3 T water
1 T sesame oil

PREPARATION:

Clean, shell, and de-vein 12 large raw prawns (or shrimp). Cut in half lengthwise. Place the prawns in a bowl and add 1 T rice wine, 1 T cornstarch, and a dash of salt, mix well until coated. Heat the wok, add 3 T cup canola oil, and bring to high heat. Add the prawn mixture, stir-fry for 2 min or until the prawns change color. Remove with slotted spoon or a wire skimmer and drain. Remove the oil from the wok and return 1 T of the reserved oil. Reheat the wok, add 1 t chopped ginger root, 1 T chopped green onion, 2 T chopped presoaked wood ears, 1 sliced  Chinese cucumber, and 1 T rice wine, stir-fry 30 sec. Add the prawns and mix well. In a separate bowl, combine 3 T water and 1 T cornstarch until dissolved. Add to the wok, cook until the sauce thickens. Add a dash of sesame oil; transfer to serving platter and serve at once.

SHANGHAI STIR-FRIED RICE CAKES
上海炒年糕

STIR-FRIED RICE CAKES WITH SHREDDED PORK (SHANGHAI STYLE)

INGREDIENTS:

6 oz shredded pork loin
12 oz rice cakes (nian gao, large, thick noodle slices)
1 T soy sauce
1 t rice wine
1 t cornstarch
3 T canola oil
2 T shredded pickled mustard greens
1 cup shredded Chinese cabbage
1/4 t salt
2 T water or stock

PREPARATION:

Bring 6 cups water to boil in the stock pot, add 12 oz rice cakes (nian gao, large, thick noodle slices), and cook for 3 min or until the cakes rise to the surface. Place 6 oz shredded pork in a bowl and add 1 T soy sauce, 1 t rice wine, and 1 t cornstarch. Mix well until coated. Heat the wok, add 3 T canola oil and bring to high heat. Add the pork mixture and stir-fry until cooked through. Remove with a slotted spoon or a wire skimmer. Reheat the remaining oil and add 2 T shredded pickled mustard greens, 1 cup shredded Chinese cabbage and stir-fry until heated through. Add 1/4 t salt or to taste and 2 T water or stock and mix well. Add the precook rice cakes and stir-fry for 2 min. Remove to serving plate, serve immediately.

SHRIMP FRIED RICE
蝦仁炒飯
FRIED RICE WITH SHRIMP AND EGG (CANTONESE)

INGREDIENTS:

3 cup precooked rice
1/2 lb medium raw shrimp shells and veins removed
1/4 t salt or to taste
1 t cornstarch
1 t rice wine
1/2 cup chopped brown onion
1 T chopped green onion
1/4 cup precooked green peas

2 T precooked diced carrot
1/4 cup diced ham
1 T soy sauce
3 eggs, beaten
1/4 cup canola oil
1/2 t salt
1 T rice wine (or water)
1/4 t white pepper powder

PREPARATION:

In a bowl, beat 3 eggs with 1 T rice wine, a dash of salt, and 1 t canola oil. Heat the wok, add 1/4 cup canola oil. Add the egg mixture by pouring it very slowly into the hot oil. When the egg mixture becomes puffy and light, remove the eggs from the wok with a slotted spoon to a separate plate. Remove the oil from the wok and reserve. Place 1/2 lb medium raw shrimp, veins and shells removed in a bowl, add 1/4 t salt, 1 t rice wine, and 1 t cornstarch to, and mix until coated. Heat the wok, add 2 T canola oil, add the shrimp mixture and stir-fry until the shrimp

change color. Remove the shrimp with a slotted spoon or a wire skimmer and place them in a sieve set in a larger bowl to drain. Return the reserved oil to the wok and reheat it. Add 1/2 cup chopped brown onion, 1 T chopped green onion, 1/4 cup precooked green peas, 2 T precooked diced carrot, and 1/4 cup diced ham, stir-fry until hot and combined. Add 3 cups precooked rice, 1 T soy sauce, a dash of salt, a dash of white pepper powder, and stir for 30 sec. Place the eggs and the shrimp on top of the rice mixture and fold gently to break the egg sheet into small pieces. Remove to serving platter, sprinkle 1 T chopped green onion as garnish, and serve immediately.

SHRIMP WITH SPICY SALT
椒鹽蝦
SPICY SALT SHRIMP (CANTONESE)

INGREDIENTS:

3/4 lb medium size raw shrimp
1 t rice wine
1 egg white
2 T cornstarch
2 cups canola oil for frying
1 T chopped garlic

1 T chopped green onion
1 t chopped hot green chili pepper
1 t salt or to taste
1/4 t five spice powder
1/4 t Szechwan peppercorn powder
1/4 t black pepper powder

PREPARATION:

Remove the legs from 3/4 lb medium size raw shrimp leaving the shells and heads attached. Using a toothpick, carefully remove the black veins without disturbing the shells. Place the shrimp in a bowl, add 1 t rice wine, 1 egg white, 2 T cornstarch, and stir gently to coat. Heat the wok, add 2 cups canola oil, bring to high heat. Reduce the heat before adding shrimp mixture (to prevent the oil from spattering). Add the shrimp and deep-fry over high heat for 2 min or until shrimp change color. Remove the shrimp with a slotted spoon or a wire skimmer and

place them in a sieve set in a larger bowl or on paper towels to drain. Remove all oil from wok. To the almost dry wok, add 1 T chopped garlic, 1 T chopped green onion, and 1 t chopped hot green chili pepper, stir-fry until fragrant. Add 1 t salt or to taste, a dash of five spice powder, a dash of Szechwan peppercorn powder, and a dash of black pepper powder. Return the shrimp to the wok and mix until coated. Remove to serving platter, place any remaining onion/garlic/pepper mixture on top and serve immediately.

SMELTS WITH ROE

多春魚

FRIED SEASONAL SMALL FISH WITH ROE (CANTONESE)

INGREDIENTS:

12 oz small roe smelts (seasonal)
4 T flour
1/4 t baking powder
1/4 t five spice powder
1/4 t salt
1 t canola oil
1 egg
1 cup canola oil for frying
Spicy salt

PREPARATION:

Rinse and drain 12 oz small smelts with roe (available at a Chinese market or fishmonger). In a small bowl combine 4 T flour, 1/4 t baking powder, 1/4 t five spice powder, a dash of salt, 1 t canola oil, and 1 egg, mix to form a smooth batter. Add the fish and mix gently to coat (the batter should be used immediately). Heat the wok, add 1 cup canola oil and bring to high heat. Add the battered fish and deep-fry for 30 sec. Turn with spatula to separate the fish, continue to fry over medium heat for another 30 sec or until golden and crisp. Remove and drain by placing  the fish in a sieve set over another bowl or drain them on paper towels. Place on warm platter and serve with spicy salt on the side.

SPICY SALT FROG LEGS
椒鹽田雞腿
DEEP FRIED FROG LEG WITH HOT SPICY SALT (CANTONESE)

INGREDIENTS:

1 lb frog legs
1 egg white
1/4 t salt or to taste
1 T rice wine
3 T cornstarch
1 T flour
2 t five spice powder
1 t Szechwan peppercorns
1/4 t salt   1 T chopped garlic
2 T chopped green onion
1 T chopped hot red pepper

PREPARATION:

Rinse and dry 1 lb frog legs and place in a bowl. Add 1 egg white, 1 T rice wine, 3 T cornstarch, 1 T flour, and a dash of salt, mix until coated. Heat the wok and add 1 cup canola oil or enough to cover the frog legs. Deep fry at high heat for 5 min. Reduce heat to medium and continue to cook for 5 min. Reduce heat to medium and continue to cook for 5 min until golden brown. Remove the meat with a slotted spoon or a wire skimmer and place it in a sieve set in a larger bowl or on paper towels to drain. Remove the oil form wok. Reheat the almost dry wok and add 1 T chopped garlic,

2 T chopped green onion, and 1 T chopped hot red pepper. Stir-fry quickly until fragrant. Add 2 t five spice powder and 1/4 t salt or to taste, stir-fry for a few seconds more. Return the frog legs to the wok and stir quickly until coated and heated through. Place the frog legs on a warm serving platter, place any remaining garlic-chili mixture on top and serve immediately.

STIR-FRIED RICE STICK NOODLES
炒米粉

INGREDIENTS:

6 oz rice stick
4 oz shredded pork loin
3 T canola oil
2 T presoaked chopped dried shrimp
3 T presoaked shredded black mushroom
1 cup shredded cabbage or bean sprouts
1 T soy sauce
1 t cornstarch,
1/4 t sugar
1/4 t salt
1 cup chicken stock

PREPARATION:

Place 4 oz shredded pork loin in a bowl, add 1 T soy sauce, 1 t cornstarch, and mix well. Heat the wok and add 3 T canola oil. Bring to high heat and add the pork mixture. Stir-fry until the meat changes color. Remove the meat with a slotted spoon or a wire skimmer and place it in a sieve set over a larger bowl or on paper towels to drain. Reheat the remaining oil, add 2 T presoaked and chopped dried shrimp, 3 T presoaked shredded black mushroom, 1 cup shredded cabbage or bean sprouts, salt to taste, and the meat mixture, stir-fry until well mixed. Remove almost all the  cabbage and meat mixture and set aside. Reheat the wok, add 6 oz presoaked rice stick (noodles), and stir well. Add 1 cup water or chicken stock, 2 T soy sauce, and a dash of sugar. Cook carefully over high heat until stock is reduced and the noodles are almost dry (being careful not to overcook the noodles). Return the reserved cabbage mixture and stir until combined and heated through. Sprinkle with 1/4 t white pepper powder. Garnish with a few 2-inch sections of green onion.

STUFFED MUSHROOMS
釀香菇
BLACK MUSHROOMS STUFFED WITH FISH PASTE (CANTONESE)

INGREDIENTS:

8 dried black mushrooms
3 T cornstarch
3 oz ground pork
6 oz fish paste
1 T chopped green onion
1 t soy sauce
1/2 t sugar
1/4 t salt
1/4 t black pepper powder
1 T sesame oil
2 T chopped ham

PREPARATION:

Soak 8 dried black mushrooms with warm water until soft, drain and pat dry. Remove the stems and sprinkle a little cornstarch on each mushrooms cap, set aside. In the bowl, combine 3 oz ground pork, 6 oz fish paste, 1 T chopped green onion, 1 t soy sauce, 1/2 t sugar, 1/4 t salt or to taste, a dash of black pepper powder, and 1 T cornstarch, mix well. Form the mixture into 8 small balls. Press one ball gently into each mushrooms cap. Place the filled mushroom caps in 2-inch deep glass or ceramic bowl. In a saucepan or steamer large enough to hold the

bowl, add 4 cups water, place the dish with the mushroom on a rack above the water and steam for 20 min until the mushrooms are cooked through. Remove the mushrooms to a serving platter placing each on a slice of carrot and keep warm. In the small saucepan, combine 1/2 cup water and 1 T cornstarch, salt to taste, and a dash of sesame oil, cook until the sauce thickens. Pour over the stuffed mushrooms, sprinkle with chopped ham, and serve.

TARO "SHI-FAN"

芋頭粥

RICE PORRIDGE WITH TARO (HOME STYLE)

INGREDIENTS:

1 cup canola oil for frying
1 cup taro cut into 1/2-inch cubes
1 T presoaked and chopped dried shrimp
1 T dried shallot
3 oz ground pork
10 cups water
3/4 cup presoaked short grain rice
1/4 cup presoak sweet (glutinous) rice
2 T tapioca
1 T rice wine
1/4 t white pepper powder
1/4 t salt
1 T chopped Chinese celery

PREPARATION:

Heat the wok, add 1 cup canola oil, and bring to high heat. Add 1 cup taro root cut into 1/2-inch cubes and deep-fry until light brown. Remove with a slotted spoon or a wire skimmer and place in a sieve over a bowl to drain. Remove the oil from the wok and set aside. Reheat the wok, return 1 T of the reserved oil and bring to high heat. Add 1 T presoaked and chopped dried shrimp and 1 T dried shallot. Stir-fry until fragrant. Add 3 oz ground pork and stir-fry mixing well until the meat is cooked through. Add 10 cups water, 3/4 cup presoaked short grain rice, 1/4 cup presoak sweet (glutinous) rice, 2 T tapioca and the reserved taro cubes. Mix well and bring to a boil. Simmer for 45 min over low heat or until rice is cooked into porridge. Add 1 T rice wine, a dash of white pepper powder, and salt to taste, mix gently. Remove to a serving bowl. Garnish with 1 T chopped Chinese celery.

Printed in the United States
By Bookmasters